Plant Life

Theresa Greenaway

HODDER
Wayland
an imprint of Hodder
Children's Books

CYCLES IN NATURE
Other titles in this series:
Food Chains

The Water Cycle

All Wayland books encourage children to read and help them improve their literacy.

 The contents page, page numbers, headings and index help locate specific pieces of information.

 The glossary reinforces alphabetic knowledge and extends vocabulary.

✓ The further information section suggests other books and websites dealing with the same subject.

Cover: A bee sucks nectar from a flower (*main image*); (*clockwise from top right*) the fruits and seeds of a dandelion; a diagram of a flower; toadstools in the autumn sun; yew berries.
Title page: A bee sucks nectar from a flower.
Contents page: Toadstools in the autumn sun.

Series editor: Nicola Wright
Book editor: Alison Cooper
Series and cover design: Sterling Associates
Book design: Jean Wheeler

First published in 2000 by
Hodder Wayland a division of Hodder Children's Books
388 Euston Road
London NW1 3BH

© Copyright 2000 Hodder Wayland

Typeset by Jean Wheeler
Printed and bound in Italy byEurografica S.p.a.
Turin

British Library Cataloguing in Publication Data
Greenaway, Theresa
Plant Life. - (Cycles in nature)
1. Plant ecology - Juvenile literature
I. Title
581.7

ISBN 0 7502 2516 5

Picture acknowledgements
The publishers would like to thank the following for allowing their images to be used in this book: Biofotos 13, 29/Heather Angel; Bruce Coleman *cover (top left)*/Hans Reinhard, *cover (top right)*, 17 & 21/Jane Burton; NHPA 10/Hellio & Van Ingen, 11/Daniel Heuclin, 18 *(right)* Joe Blossom, 19/G. I. Bernard, 24/E. A. Janes, 27/Stephen Dalton; OSF *cover (main image) & title page*/Alastair Shay; 4 *(left)* George I. Bernard, 4 *(right)*/Daniel J. Cox, 7/John Brown, 20/Terry Andrewartha, 23/Roger Brown, 25/John McCammon; Stock Market *cover (bottom left) & contents page*, 15/Sanford & Agliolo, 22/Naideau, 28; Tony Stone Images 5/Richard Passmore, 6/Jane Gifford, 12/H. Richard Johnston, 18 *(left)*/Gary Holscher, 26/Peter Cade; Roger Vlitos 8. Wayland Picture Library 13. Artwork on pages 9 and 16 is by Peter Bull.

Contents

Plants all Around

From the smallest flower to the tallest tree, the life cycles of plants are made up of the same stages. Seeds sprout into delicate seedlings. These grow larger, producing leaves and stems or woody trunks. Eventually, they make flowers and seeds of their own. The cycle starts all over again.

▼ Only low-growing plants can survive in the cold tundra.

Wherever they grow, we depend on plants. We use them for food and medicines, and to make clothing and buildings. They release oxygen into the air which helps us to breathe. They feed our farm animals.

◀ Trees tower to great heights in the warm, damp rain forest.

Are you a plant-eater?

Make a list of all the plants that you eat in one day. Some are easy – we all know that potatoes, oranges and lettuces are plants. Others are more tricky. If you have cornflakes for breakfast, you are eating maize. Toast is made of wheat. Chocolate comes from the seeds of the cocoa tree. Did you know that chewing gum is made from the elastic sap of the chicle tree?

▼ This market stall is piled high with delicious plants that we can eat.

How a Plant Grows

Seeds can only sprout, or germinate, when conditions are just right. They need moisture, warmth and oxygen. Some seeds will only germinate in darkness, but others require some sunlight before they can start to grow. Seeds that fall from a plant in autumn lie dormant in the soil until the cold winter is over.

▼ Frost like this kills seedlings but seeds in the ground are safe.

Germination

When a seed is ready to grow, it soaks up water and swells. Its protective outer coat splits. A tiny root appears and pushes down into the soil. A tiny shoot grows up towards the light. As soon as it bursts through the soil, the shoot turns green. The first leaves unfold.

This broad ▶ bean has already developed roots and a shoot. The first leaves are about to unfold.

Which way up?

Soak some runner bean seeds in water overnight. Then cut wide strips of blotting paper and curl them round to fit inside two jam jars. Arrange two or three beans in one jar, lying 'sideways' between the paper and the glass. Put some more beans 'upright' in the other jar. Pour about 2 cm of water into the bottom of the jar so that the blotting paper is standing in water. Look at the beans every day and watch what happens to the roots and shoots.

Growth

A young plant needs water, sunshine, minerals, warmth and gases called oxygen and carbon dioxide in order to grow well. These come from the air that surrounds its shoots and leaves, and from the soil that surrounds its roots.

▲ Leaves turn yellow when they do not receive enough sunlight.

A plant can make simple sugars using carbon dioxide from the air and water from the soil. But to be able to do this, a plant also needs sunlight. The energy in sunlight is trapped by the green leaves. It provides the power to combine carbon dioxide and water to make sugar. This process is called photosynthesis.

A plant also needs minerals, such as nitrates, phosphates and potassium. These minerals come from the soil. They dissolve in water and are taken up by the plant's roots.

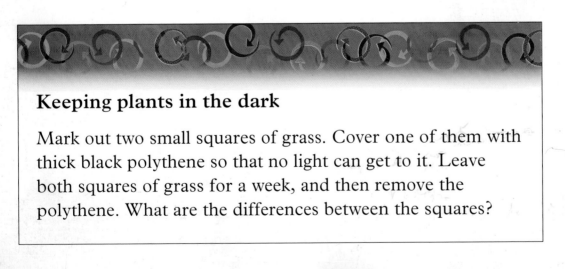

Keeping plants in the dark

Mark out two small squares of grass. Cover one of them with thick black polythene so that no light can get to it. Leave both squares of grass for a week, and then remove the polythene. What are the differences between the squares?

During the process of making sugar, the plant forms a waste product – oxygen. This gas leaves the plant and goes into the air. There is always plenty of oxygen in the air for people and animals to breathe because it is being released from plants all the time. Plants also need oxygen but they only use a small amount.

▼ A magnified view of the inside of a leaf.

Sunlight

Surface of leaf

Water passes from the leaf veins into the cells.

A green pigment in the cells traps the energy in sunlight.

The leaves absorb sunlight.

Carbon dioxide enters the leaf through tiny holes.

Oxygen and water vapour are released.

Water travels through the roots and up the stem.

◄ This diagram shows how photosynthesis takes place.

How well does a plant grow without leaves?

Find two plants of the same species that are about the same height. Remove all the leaves from one, but do not remove the bud right at the top. Keep the plants in the same place and make sure they are watered. Compare the growth of these two plants over several weeks.

▼ These sunflowers have been planted in rows so that the sunlight can reach each plant.

A healthy plant soon produces one or more stems and plenty of green leaves. If you look down on a plant from above, you can see that its leaves are arranged so that as much sunlight falls upon each one as possible. The greater the amount of sunlight each leaf receives, the more sugar the plant can make.

Roots

Hidden underground, a network of roots spreads through the soil. The roots hold the plant firmly in the ground. Water and dissolved minerals enter the roots through the tiny root tips. The more roots a plant has, the more water and minerals it can take up.

Mangroves are trees that grow ▶ along tropical coasts. Parts of their roots are above ground and they absorb oxygen from the air.

Food stores

Some roots and stems are also used as a food store. All through the summer, the plant makes more sugar than it needs. The sugar is turned into starch and stored in swollen underground stems and roots. In winter, the leafy shoots die down. Next spring, the plant uses its food reserves to provide the energy for new buds to start growing.

Flowers

Most kinds of plant produce flowers. We enjoy looking at their attractive blooms, but the purpose of all flowers is to help the plant to reproduce successfully.

▲ This tiger lily has colourful petals and orange stamens. The yellow-tipped carpel is surrounded by the stamens.

Looking at the parts of a flower

Collect some different kinds of flower. There may be some growing in your school playground, or in your garden. (Check with your teacher or parent that it is safe to pick them.) Carefully take each flower apart, and try to work out which are the parts shown in the diagram opposite. You may find it helpful to use a magnifying glass.

Parts of a flower

The female reproductive organ is called the carpel. At the top is the stigma.

The petals attract insects and other animals to pollinate the flower.

The stamens are the male reproductive organs. The stamen has a slender stalk with a sac (the anther) containing pollen at the tip. Each tiny pollen grain contains a minute male sex cell.

A short stalk (the style) leads to the ovary.

The ovary contains one or more ovules, each with a tiny female sex cell.

Sepals enclose and protect the flower whilst it is in bud. When the bud starts to open the sepals fold back and may drop off.

▲ This diagram shows the different parts of a flower.

Reproduction

A plant reproduces by making seeds that will grow
into new plants of the same kind. Pollination is
the first stage in plant reproduction. Pollen
is carried from the stamens of one flower to
the stigma of another.

Wind pollination

Some flowers are pollinated by
the wind. These flowers have
tiny, often greenish petals,
with no nectar or scent
because they do not need to
attract insects and birds. The
stamens stick out on long, thin
stalks. When the pollen sacs
split, the fine, dusty pollen is
blown away. Most of it is
wasted because it simply lands
on the ground. But some
lands on the stigma of exactly
the same kind of flower.

◄ A fine cloud of pollen is
released from the catkins of a
silver birch tree.

Animal pollination

Other types of flower are pollinated by insects, birds, or small mammals, such as bats. Bees and butterflies are attracted by flowers with colourful petals, sweet scents and nectar. They drink the nectar and feed on the pollen. Some of the sticky pollen clings to the insects' hairy bodies. When the insects fly to other flowers, this pollen sticks to the stigmas, and the flowers are pollinated.

Which flowers attract most insects?

If you have flowers growing in your school playground or your garden, watch carefully to see which kinds of insect visit them – bees, butterflies or tiny flies. Some flowers attract far more insects than others. Why do you think this is?

As the hummingbird ▶ drinks nectar from the flower, pollen clings to its beak and feathers.

Fertilization

Fertilization takes place when a male sex cell fuses, or joins, with a female sex cell. For this to happen in a flowering plant, the male sex cell has to travel from the pollen grain right down into the ovary of the female part of the flower.

1. A pollen grain of the right kind lands on a stigma and sprouts a very tiny tube. This is too small to see unless it is magnified under a microscope.

2. The tiny tube grows down the style and into the ovary.

3. Eventually, it reaches a minute egg, or ovule. The male sex cell travels down the tube. When it reaches the ovule, it enters and fuses with the female sex cell inside. Now the ovule has been fertilized. It can develop into a seed.

◀ This diagram shows how fertilization takes place.

Seed development

As the seed starts to develop, other changes take place. The petals fall from the flower. The ovary gets bigger. It is now known as a fruit. A fruit may contain just one seed, or many seeds. The seeds are completely enclosed and protected by the fruit, and are attached to its wall by tiny stalks. Sugars and other food pass through this stalk and into the growing seed.

▲ You can see the brown remains of the flower on this rose tree. The red rose hips are not the actual fruits; the fruits are inside them.

Fruits and seeds

We think of a fruit as something that is juicy and sweet to eat – like a peach or a raspberry. But some foods that we think of as vegetables, such as tomatoes, aubergines and cucumbers, are really fruits. Many other kinds of fruit are dry or leathery. These are often known as seed cases.

▲ Sweet cherry trees produce juicy fruits; horse chestnuts produce prickly green ones. Inside the horse chestnut are shiny brown seeds – the 'conkers'.

How many fruits and seed cases can you find?

Autumn is a good time to look for different types of fruit and seed cases. Some fruits and seeds are poisonous, so always check with a teacher or parent before collecting them. Carefully cut them open if they are soft, or pull them apart. Draw pictures of each fruit, and the seeds it contains. You might need to use a magnifying glass.

Spreading without seeds

Some plants can reproduce without making seeds.
One way of doing this is by sending out long stems
which creep over the surface of the ground. At the
tip of each stem, a new little plantlet develops. It
makes shoots and leaves, and sends tiny, new roots
down into the ground.

New strawberry plantlets form at ▶
the end of long, creeping stems.

Seed dispersal

Imagine what would happen if all the seeds that a plant produced simply fell to the ground below. When the seeds germinated, there would not be enough space, light or water for all the young plants to survive. Most would die. To prevent this, plants spread their seeds far and wide. This is called seed dispersal.

Inside berries, there are small seeds that have tough seed coats. When a bird swallows a berry, the seeds pass through the bird unharmed. They land on the ground in the bird's droppings, often a long way away from the parent plant.

◀ The bright colours of berries attract birds to feed on them.

Gorse and laburnum spread their seeds by shooting them explosively into the air. These plants have fruits that slowly dry out, until the fruit wall splits into two halves. Each half immediately twists into a spiral, flicking out all the seeds.

Some fruits and seeds are carried away from the parent plant by the wind. Sycamore and ash trees have winged fruits that contain one or two seeds. As they fall, the wings help the fruits to spin slowly to the ground. By the time they land, they have drifted away from the parent plant.

The dandelion ▶ produces many fruits, each containing a single seed. They float away on the lightest breeze.

Recycling

In cooler parts of the world, plants die down and deciduous trees shed their leaves before the cold winter arrives. In tropical regions which have a long dry season, trees shed their leaves to save water. Many nutrients are locked up inside dead leaves. Before they can be released and returned to the soil, the dead plant material has to be broken down.

▲ Leaf litter lies in a thick layer on the floor of a wood.

Nature's recyclers

Dead plants and fallen leaves are broken down by animals, fungi and bacteria. Animals such as earthworms and millipedes eat dead plants and leaves. Fungi and bacteria grow on dead leaves, and rot dead wood. Eventually, all that is left is a dark brown, crumbly compost. All the ingredients that made up the living plant have been recycled by other organisms or have soaked back into the soil to be absorbed by new plants.

▼ Dead wood rots as fungi use the nutrients from it to help them grow.

What lives in leaf litter?

Collect damp leaf litter in trays and take it back to your classroom. Look carefully for small insects, spiders, worms, centipedes, millipedes and slugs. Some of these feed on the leaf litter, but others are hunters, preying on other small creatures. Take care – some can bite! Remember to put these small animals back where they came from and to wash your hands after handling them.

Human Interference

People grow plants for food but this can often interfere with natural plant cycles. Unwanted plants are removed and farmers use various methods to produce large quantities of healthy crops as quickly as possible.

Killing weeds

In natural grassland, many different kinds of plant grow together. But a farmer does not want variety. A farmer just wants to grow one kind of plant in each field. Any other plants growing amongst the crop are weeds, competing for light, water and nutrients.

Most farmers today spray herbicides to kill weeds. But this means that some wildflowers that grow as weeds among crops have become very rare.

▼ Until the mid-twentieth century wildflowers such as poppies often grew among crops like this.

Pesticides

Insect pests that eat crops do not have to search far for their food plants because they are surrounded by them. Pests multiply quickly and eat more and more of the farmer's crop. To prevent this, the farmer sprays the plants with pesticides. Unfortunately, these often kill harmless insects as well as pests.

A farmer ▶
sprays his
cabbage crop
to protect it
from pests.

Fertilizers

Growing a crop takes a lot of minerals from the soil. When the plants are harvested they are taken away instead of being broken down naturally so that nutrients can return to the soil. The farmer has to use fertilizers to replace the nutrients. When rain washes excess fertilizer into lakes and rivers it upsets the natural chemical balance in them. Outbreaks of bacteria that feed on the enriched water can poison fish and birds.

Breeding new crops

The first farmers started to grow wheat and barley over 10,000 years ago. Their crops were very different from those planted today. They were much more like wild grasses, with small grains and seed heads that shattered, scattering the precious grain over the ground.

The early farmers saved seed from the best plants to sow the next year. By selecting the best in this way, crop plants gradually became bigger and better. They became less and less like their wild ancestors. Over the centuries, for example, cultivated apples became larger, juicier and sweeter than wild crab apples.

▲ The seed heads of today's cereal crops do not break up until they are threshed, so none of the grain is lost.

In the twentieth century, scientists began to unravel the mysteries of genetics – how plants pass on their characteristics when they reproduce. Now plant breeders can make genetically modified organisms (GMOs). Genetic material from one kind of organism is put into the genetic material of a quite different species. This can give a crop completely new characteristics. For example, it may develop its own chemicals that poison insect pests.

GMOs sound as though they may be a good idea, but many people are worried that they may not be safe to eat. No one knows exactly what effects they will have on wildlife.

▼ In parts of the USA, monarch butterfly caterpillars have died after feeding on plants dusted with pollen from genetically modified maize.

Habitat loss

Forests have been felled, natural grasslands ploughed up and wetlands drained, to make more room for people to live and work. In the Everglades of the USA, for example, canals and pumps built to prevent coastal cities from flooding have altered the wetland environment. Hundreds of plant species have been badly affected.

Disappearing species

Other plants have become scarce because they have been cut down or removed for use by people. So many Brazilian rosewood trees have been cut down for their fine timber that this tree is now very rare. Plant collectors pay local people to collect orchids from tropical rain forests, and bulbs such as cyclamens from mountain slopes. This has pushed some species to the brink of extinction.

Any human activity that reduces the diversity of the world's plants also affects the insects, birds and other animals that depend upon them. We run the risk of losing plants that may contain substances we could one day use as medicines. We will also make our planet a less attractive place for future generations.

▲ Thieves stole plants of this rare orchid from Kinabalu Park in Malaysia.

◄ Swampy habitats like the Everglades of Florida, USA, are becoming rare.

Plants in danger?

All round the world, different kinds of plant are in danger of dying out. Use books, CD-Roms and the Internet to find out which plants are at risk in your country. What threatens these plants? What do you think can be done to save them?

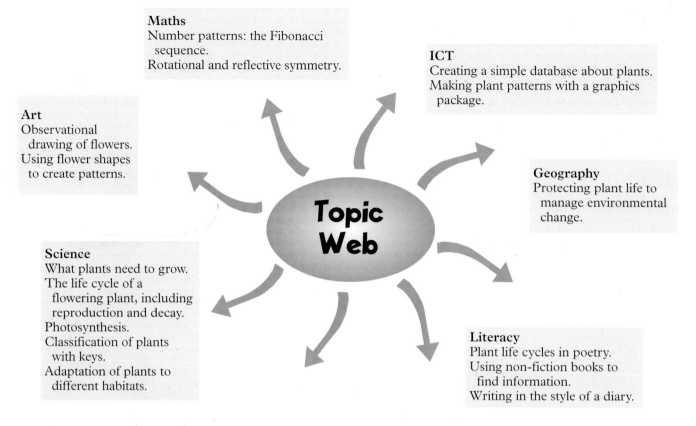

Maths
Number patterns: the Fibonacci
   sequence.
Rotational and reflective symmetry.

ICT
Creating a simple database about plants.
Making plant patterns with a graphics
   package.

Art
Observational
   drawing of flowers.
Using flower shapes
   to create patterns.

Geography
Protecting plant life to
   manage environmental
   change.

Topic Web

Science
What plants need to grow.
The life cycle of a
   flowering plant, including
   reproduction and decay.
Photosynthesis.
Classification of plants
   with keys.
Adaptation of plants to
   different habitats.

Literacy
Plant life cycles in poetry.
Using non-fiction books to
   find information.
Writing in the style of a diary.

More Activities

Literacy
• Use non-fiction books to make short fact-files about
  different species of plant. Don't forget to use contents
  lists and indexes to find the information you need.
• Many poems use the idea of plant life cycles. Two that
  you might like to read are Philip Larkin's 'The Trees'
  and Robert Frost's 'In Hardwood Groves'.
• Write the diary of a mystery plant over a year. Include
  clues such as the colour of its flowers (if it has them),
  when it flowers and what kinds of seed it produces.
  Get your friends to guess which plant you have
  written about?

Maths
• Use patterns you have made in art to investigate
  reflectional and rotational symmetry.

Science
• With the help of an adult, explore a small patch of
  ground about 30 cm x 30 cm, in a field, park, garden or
  the school grounds. Look carefully at the plants growing
  there, and describe and draw them. Use the information
  you have collected to identify all the plants growing in
  the plot of land.

Geography
• Investigate plants in a particular environment, such as a
  rain forest. Find out why we should protect this
  environment and make a poster to explain the reasons to
  other people.

ICT
• Use a graphics package to draw a simple plant picture.
  Use the package to transform the picture in different
  ways and make a recurring pattern.
• Use the data you collected in your study of a small plot
  of land to make a simple database, showing which plants
  occurred most and least frequently.

Art
• Look closely at a flower and try to draw or paint exactly
  what you see. Can you include the main parts of the
  flower (see page 13) in your drawing?
• Investigate wallpaper or wrapping paper which uses a
  recurring picture of leaves or flowers. How is the picture
  arranged? Design your own picture and arrange it in a
  recurring pattern.

Glossary

bacteria Tiny living things that can only be seen using a microscope.

deciduous tree A tree that loses its leaves each autumn.

diversity Variety.

dormant Inactive or 'sleeping'. A dormant plant is not dead but is waiting for the right conditions before it starts to grow.

habitats The particular places where plants and animals live.

leaf litter Dead leaves that are being broken down into small pieces.

life cycle The stages that all living things go through from birth, through growth and reproduction to death.

nectar A sugary liquid produced by some flowers.

nutrients Substances that living things need to take in to help them grow.

oxygen A gas in the air that plants and animals (including humans) need in order to survive.

pollen The fine powder containing the male sex cell of a plant.

rain forest Thick forest that grows in areas where the weather is hot all year round.

reproduce To produce a new living thing.

seedlings Young plants.

species A group of plants or animals that share the same features and can breed with each other.

tundra The cold, treeless lands of the far north of America, Europe and Asia.

Further Information

BOOKS

I Didn't Know That...Some Plants Grow in Mid-Air by Claire Llewellyn (Watts, 1997)

Nature and Science: Leaves by Taylor Burton (Watts, 1997)

Straightforward Science: Plant Life by Peter Riley (Watts, 1998)

The Earth Strikes Back: Plant Life by Pamela Grant and Arthur Haswell (Belitha Press, 1999)

WEBSITES

www.foe.co.uk Friends of the Earth

www.rbgkew.org.uk Royal Botanical Gardens, Kew

www.soilassoc@gnapc.org.uk Soil Association

www.nhm.ac.uk The Natural History Museum

www.gnapc.org./pesticidetrust The Pesticide Trust

Index

Page numbers printed in **bold** mean that there is information about this topic in a photograph, diagram or caption.